DAVID WHYTE

STILL POSSIBLE

BOOKS BY DAVID WHYTE

POETRY

Songs for Coming Home

Where Many Rivers Meet

Fire in the Earth

The House of Belonging

Everything is Waiting for You

River Flow: New and Selected Poems

Pilgrim

*The Sea in You: Twenty Poems of
Requited and Unrequited Love*

The Bell and the Blackbird

David Whyte: Essentials

PROSE

*The Heart Aroused:
Poetry and the Preservation of the Soul
in Corporate America*

*Crossing the Unknown Sea:
Work as a Pilgrimage of Identity*

*The Three Marriages:
Reimagining Work, Self and Relationship*

*Consolations:
The Solace, Nourishment and
Underlying Meaning
of Everyday Words*

DAVID WHYTE

Still Possible

20 22

MANY RIVERS PRESS
LANGLEY, WASHINGTON

www.davidwhyte.com

First published in 2022
by Many Rivers Press
PO Box 868
Langley, WA 98260
USA

A catalog record for this book
is available from
the Library of Congress

ISBN 978-1-932887-55-6

Printed in
the United States of America

First printing 2021

For Edward: A close friend through long years, a patient conversationalist through all troubles, and a brother in the endless mountains.

Contents

STILL POSSIBLE

NARRATIVES

BEGINNING

For the Road to Santiago

For the road to Santiago,
don't make new declarations
about what to bring
and what to leave behind.

Bring what you have.

You were always going
that way anyway,
you were always
going there all along.

Perfectly Made

The first illusion to face
is that your structured,
too easily understandable world
is a world that will keep you safe,
that naming everything and everyone
in such small ways can protect you from
the larger ways the world was made
to undo you; that you can slip by
the larger, intuited, necessary
and unavoidable act of letting go,
without being noticed, without
being seen and without being made
to look; that your inevitable
and necessary and eventually
surprising disappearance
can be kept at bay by refusing to live
fully in a body wounded by the
very act of being born.

The second illusion
is that you were never made
to have your heart
broken even once,
never mind
again and again.

To break through
the second illusion
might be to understand
you were made

to attract the right kind
of peril, to understand
you were perfectly made
for the fullness
of every humiliation
you have ever experienced
and that, above all,
at the bottom
of each humiliation,
you were most perfectly
made for every single
intimate falling apart
you have ever endured
in your brief history.

The third illusion
is that
you are not
equal
to everything
listed above.

The third illusion
is that you were not
perfectly made
in every way
to undo the first illusion.

PERFECTLY MADE *Some dynamics have to be addressed head on, in a declarative voice, in what I have often called 'the poetry of self-admonition'. Despite the constant need for self-compassion, there is also a place for giving our self a good telling off, for cornering and holding to account our illusive, free floating, surface personality and bringing it firmly and convincingly to ground.*

You Know When It's Time to Go

You know
when it's time to go:

that involuntary
sense
of hesitation
discovered
inside
what only looks
like your
own body,

a hesitation
like a movement
in itself.

Your reluctance
to hear
the call
as much
an invitation
as if
a door
had opened

in the broad
heavens
and called
you through.

Your unwillingness
to hear the
birdsong
another kind
of listening,

and
the complete
inability
to speak

such a clear
and articulate
understanding
of what you
want.

Even in the midst
of thinking
you'll
never be ready

even when
you feel
you have never
deserved
that freedom
to go

even under
the comforting
illusion
that you
never had
a single speck
of faith
in what you want

you have
already packed
your silent
reluctance away,
lifted your ear
to the morning
birdsong

and before
anyone
can wake

you are
out the door,
down the road
round the corner
and on your way.

YOU KNOW WHEN IT'S TIME TO GO *Written with a good but far away friend in mind, going through the agonies of a possible separation. In any leaving of course, the real mystery always lies in coming to understand what kind of leaving we are involved with, sometimes we have to be 'out the door' to leave our old, uninvolved self behind, in order to take the relationship deeper. Sometimes we actually have to cut the physical ties that bind to leave the present dynamic. Either way, the necessary agony involved in getting to the experience is always worth the freedom bequeathed by the benefit of a full revelation.*

Beyond Santiago

Death is so simple,
one moment
you are alive
and then,
you are not.

And that fear
you carry with you
might be
equally as simple too,

that you'll
never have
the time
to accomplish
what you wish.

But stop
a moment now,
before the way
beyond,
and let me
tell you this.

You will go
out of this life
however
untimely,
having completed

every single thing
you wished.

You will
arrive
in that night like
a newborn child
welcomed
by
loving arms.

You will find
in that long
anticipated
enemy,
the ultimate form
of forgiveness
and
friendship.

Every
fearful goodbye
suddenly become,
a gentle
getting to know,

a getting to know
of a forgiveness
that was strangely

always anticipated,
a welcome
and a full understanding
of all you ever did,

everything you gave
and everything
you were given,
and then everything
you could never give,
and above all
everything you
could never
bring yourself
to receive,

those unattainable
distances
that always
broke your heart
and the gifted
understanding
of why it was so hard
for you to love,

and then
and most importantly
and right to the heart,

everything you were
and everything you gave,
that was never,
ever on your list.

BEYOND SANTIAGO *If you were to ask me in the busy, lighted hours of the day whether I believed in an after-life I would have to say that I am firmly neutral on the matter, with an accompanying practical sense, passed down from my father's Yorkshire, that we will all find out soon enough. But every now and again in the deeper states of attention and letting go, necessary to the writing of good poetry, there emerges a physical sense of a deeper and surer foundation in the body and beneath even that, a voice from an inner, tidal core identity, which displays absolutely no neutrality at all.*

INVISIBLE

Your Prayer

only began
with words,

each one
you realize,

just
a hand
on the door
to silence,

even
in your
gathered
chanted strength

what you said
in the end
was only
a shoulder
against the grain
of wood

trying to keep
the entrance
open,

until that door
which
had been no door
at all
gave in

to necessary
grief,
which is really
only the full
understanding
of what
you were missing
all along,
which

is really
just that
vulnerability
you needed
to make
a proper
invitation,

which is really
just you
admitting

the full depth
of your love at last.

The heart-broken
heart
coming to
heart-felt rest

the opening
inside you
now filled to the
gleaming brim
and
casting
its generous beam,

the part of you
you thought
was foolish,
the wisest voice of all.

YOUR PRAYER *This poem marks an experience, that in many ways initiated the whole cycle of experiences laid out so physically in this book; witnessing the death-bed monologue of a monk at Mount Saint Bernard Abbey, in the North of England, saying he had 'given up' praying years ago. The first thought, in witnessing his testimony, was that he had lost his faith - only to hear him then say that he had given up praying because his whole life had become a living, breathing prayer, that he had lived and indeed breathed from the atmosphere of prayer for years, whether that atmosphere was given words or not.*

Invisible

Always beside you,
always with you,
a hairsbreadth
that is no
hairsbreadth
at all.

Just a word away,
or sometimes
when the need
is great
an entire
sentence
lived fully
and physically
to the end.

But most of the time
apprehended
and even
fully realized
only
in the moment
before anything
that needs
a single word
takes shape.

Your entire body
flooded

with the gift
that is given
everyday
just
by breathing
in.

And then
the moment
you let it go,
completely
and utterly
in the out breath,
the entire world
flooded

by everything
that lies beneath
what
you had previously
thought
was you.

INVISIBLE *The poem itself follows an invisible line, between breathing in and breathing out, between saying and not saying, between experiencing and not experiencing, which, if truth be told is the unspoken frontier where all real conversations and all real relationships occur. Hence our difficulties.*

Admit

Admit,
your distant love affair
is with yourself,
and that

no one
can play
harder to get:

the unwritten letters,
the plays for time,
the heartbreak
over never being
properly answered.

That coy look
of false seduction
in the mirror,
or that hard look

to hide
what should not
be hidden.

The invitation
to undoing,
and to allowing
yourself to want
at last

what you feel
you never deserved,

the fervent wish
to come closer,

and the loving
word
of understanding
you say
to yourself
when you finally admit
to it all,
the only declaration
that counts.

ADMIT *At each new epoch of a life, we always meet the new 'you' looking back in the mirror, as a fatal stranger to whom we are surprisingly and irresistibly bound no matter our wish to turn away. I thought I would take a deeper look at this beckoning relationship, as tumultuous and as dramatic in its own way as any outer love affair.*

The Gleam

Sometimes,
in the midst
of every difficult
and everyday
awkward
way you try to
make your
onward way,

sometimes
sitting down
at the edge
of everything
that has made you
too tired
to take
another step

there's that
caught sight,
now here,
now gone

of a half imagined
wavering light
just among
the trees

just a gleam
or a wisp

of white gold
in the dying sun

a strange kind
of beckoning,

an ache
outlined
so intimately
as it is,
against
all of the doings
you have
labeled
so lovingly
as sins,

the place you
should have gone
all those years ago
still, it seems,
willing
to invite you again,

simpler this time,
not too far away

touchable now,
and within reach

just a single step
on the other side
of what you always
come to call
in the end,
forgiveness.

What is this
beguiling reluctance
to be happy?

This quickness
in turning away
the moment
you might
arrive?

The felt sense,
that a moment's
unguarded joy
might after all,
just kill you?

You know
so very well
the edge
of darkness
you have
always
carried with you.

You know
so very well,
your childhood legacy:
that particular,
inherited
sense of hurt,

given to you
so freely
by the world
you entered.

And you know
too well
by now
the body's
hesitation
at the invitation
to undo
everything
others seemed
to want to
make you learn.

But your edge
of darkness
has always
made
its own definition
secretly
as an edge of light

and the door
you closed
might,
by its very nature
be

one just waiting
to be leant against
and opened.

And happiness
might just
be a single step away,
on the other side
of that next
unhelpful
and undeserving
thought.

Your way home,
understood now,
not as an achievement,
but as a giving up,
a blessed undoing,
an arrival
in the body
and a full rest
in the give
and take
of the breath.

This living
breathing body
always waiting
to greet you

at the door,
always
no matter
the long years
you've been
away,
still
wanting you
to come home.

Pure Absence

What would
the radiant
sound of
a Red-winged
Blackbird be,
without the
extraordinary
power of your ears?

What would
the pale,
sailing moon
look like
without your
astonishing eyes?

What would your love
even know
what to do
with itself,
without
the ache
you intuit
in inevitable loss?

And who is it
comes to life
in you again
and again,

and every time
as a new miracle,
on the other side
of grief?

And then
there is this:
if you had
not come
into this world
just as you are,
and just in the way
you came,
could anyone
anywhere
ever
have lived your life
in your stead?

And then the question
toward the end
that might be
no end at all,

is there anything
or anyone
you meet
after death

you will
recognize?

No easy answer
to the
really, really beautiful
questions
of life,

they are just
the everyday
hidden invitations
that have always been
made to you,
something beckoning
you to understand
through every day
of your living
and your dying,

no possible
resolution
·you could
ever make sense of,
except
to begin every
question
in wonder.

As Meister Eckhart was
at some pains to tell us.

What you seek,
is nowhere to be found
by answering
questions.

God's full presence
felt
only in the absolute
essence
of absence.

PURE ABSENCE *This is an instance of one good friendship leading to another. The thirteenth century Dominican theologian, Meister Eckhart's answer, of 'Nowhere' to the heartfelt question: 'Where is God?' - I first heard from my friend and fellow enquirer, John O'Donohue, over dinner, as we looked out of a broad window over the mountainous heart of Connemara. The sense that human beings make their way home through the bodily ache of absence has always been part of my own understanding, so that evening, in passing on the answer 'Nowhere' John took my hand and put it into the companionable and merciful hand of Eckhart, who has been a good friend to me ever since.*

It happens to those
who live alone
that they feel sure
of visitors
when no one else
is there,

until the one day
and the one
particular
hour
working in the
quiet garden,

when they realize
at once
that all along
they have been
an invitation
to everything
and every kind
of trouble

and that life
happens by
to those who
inhabit
silence

like the bees
visiting
the tall mallow
on their legs of gold,
or the wasps
going from door to door
in those tall forests
made
so easily
by the daisies.

I have my freedom
today
because nothing
really happened
and nobody came
to see me,

only the slow
growing of the garden
in the summer heat

and the silence of that
unborn life
making itself
known at my desk,

my hands
still
dark

with the crumbling
soil
as I write
and watch

the first lines
of a new poem
like flowers
of scarlet fire
coming to fullness
in a clear light.

The Shyness of Love

Today, walking
toward each
other,
saying
'I love you'
again,
half
in recognition,
half
as strangers,

you might
not know
who you see.

Because
I've decided,
when
we meet again
today,
not to be a stranger
to love's
unsettling
and
never-ending ache
and to say
the words
again
to you

as shyly
and as nervously
as I
said them
for the first time.

Today
I have decided
to become negligent
of my fears:
I have decided
to stop
being their father
and their mother,
and to let them
be free
to find a home
in the world
wherever
they would like.

Today I am going
to walk as if coming
to meet you,
but not caring
about the way
I look
or where I find myself
from hour to hour
or day to day.

Today I am going
to forego
the long
dull hours
of the day
and turn
shyly
toward what
has always
dazzled me.

Today, with you
I am going
to teach myself
in that shyness
how to sit
in love's radiance.

And when
I am ready,
I will follow
that radiance
along every
beckoning
path.

Today,
you might look
at me

and see someone
you have never
seen before.

Today
I might live
so completely
but therefore
so invisibly
within the seamless
parallel of love's
eternal presence
you might almost
brush right
by me,

but
not before
having seen
and having
recognized
and having
understood
so shyly
and so intimately,

the tiny everyday
miracle way
we were able
to bless each
other
in passing.

THE SHYNESS OF LOVE *There is a certain appropriate shyness that we find all too familiar when we first meet someone new to whom we we are deeply and fatally attracted. But there is also the more difficult and rarely named shyness we can feel with someone we have lived with for years. Taking a relationship deeper by diving below the barrier of that learned shyness might be more difficult, but perhaps more rewarding, than overcoming the first shiver of trepidation we felt in first meeting them.*

Your Dark Offering

In your dark offering, in your half revealed
and waiting source, in your most intimate
internal essence, I find a silvered, inviting
elegance and a beautiful, and newly
confiding secrecy combined.

I find my self losing myself in you as if
in some other possible future self,
as if everything has always been waiting
for me in you, in a deep and dazzling,
unexplored nearness, as if someone

waiting at the core of you is anticipating
my arrival in the small hours of your night,
someone who would know me by my first
appearance, if only in a shadowed outline,
by my touch, my breath, my whispered words,
about to touch deep inside you, what I was
afraid until now could never be touched in me.

THE WELL

The Well

But the miracle had come simply
from allowing yourself to know
that this time you had found it,
that some now familiar stranger
appearing from far inside you,
had decided not to walk past
it anymore; that the miracle
had come in the kneeling to drink
and the prayer you said,
and the tears you shed
and the memories you held
and the realization that in this silence
you no longer had to keep
your eyes and ears averted
from the place that could save you,
and that you had the strength
at last to let go of that thirsty,
unhappy, dust-laden
pilgrim-self that brought you here,
walking with her bent back,
her bowed head
and her careful explanations.

No, the miracle had already
happened before you stood up,
before you shook off the dust
and walked along the road
beyond the well, out of the desert
and on, toward the mountain,
as if home again, as if you

deserved to have everything
you had loved all along,
as if just remembering the first
fresh taste of that clear cool spring
could lift up your face
to the morning light and set you free.

Sharing the Grail
(For Arnold and Steven)

When we arrive, and sooner
than we think, at that final goodbye
we seem to have anticipated so clearly.

When we arrive at the place
we have understood until now,
only through distance.

When we sit at the bedside
of the loved one as if sitting
by a well where we drink
from the source of all memory;

when we sip together from the grail
of that common memory
and we taste an essence
of love from that memory
that until now we could never fully say,

we are getting ready to be ready
to give the goodbye
we came all along to give.

And if our faith
and the vulnerability
of that faith,
and the wounded
nature of that faith

is felt finally and fully
at the side of that well,
we find ourselves
speaking completely and utterly
the love that we thought had
turned only to memory.

So that after the words
of goodbye are said
everything around us
in the quiet room
and everything spreading
out from the room
becomes like the well itself,
holding the same sacred water,
which is never just still water,
but a hidden flow always arriving,

a never-ending invitation
to drink from the depths,

and perhaps, most of all,
an invitation to somehow rest
in those depths: to rest in that love
that you spoke and they heard,

to wave confusion goodbye,
as you enter
the hallway of presence,

to accompany them
as you always wanted
to accompany them,

and then, to bring everyone
they loved with you,
those you have loved too
and even, those you tried to
and could not,

and then, to make room
inside you, for every single guest.

And above all to be generous now,
as you pass around the grail
of water, saying,

'This will do.
For now and for eternity.'

SHARING THE GRAIL *At its best, the bedside of a dying loved one has always been experienced as both a place of forgiveness and understanding and then a letting go, even of that hard-won understanding; leading onward then, to some astonishing threshold of freedom. Whether there is a merciful life beyond or just a full and equally merciful disappearance, drinking from the atmosphere of that forgiveness and self-understanding at the bedside and remembering all the equally beautiful memories that need no forgiveness at all, is like drinking from a deep, and nourishing source; and in the holy atmosphere of death's imminence, like the passing round of a grail.*

Intimate Invitation

I just have to look
and I see,
I just have to listen
and I hear,

I need only
the slightest desire
for anything
to find,
it has already
been met,
right
at the centre
of my body.

No need to go
anywhere
it seems and

'Not much to live for'
you say.

But you forget
how you once
saw so clearly
the brave outline
of a single leaf.

You forget
how you
were ravished
each morning
by the presence
of birdsong.

How the stream
of clouds in the sky
seemed to run
right through you,

and the sun
on your skin
seemed to
pass right
through
to some
inner complexion.

How, even when
you were stuck,
without faith,
held back
and afraid to move
even a little
you could be like
the beauty
we see in winter ice,

just
beginning to
break and flow.

And because
after all this time
you have lived
for so long without faith
in your own joys
and your own grief

you live daily
with the loss
of every word
equal to describing
what first brought
you
into this life
and the mercy
that hides
your journey
thereafter.

You live daily,
saying 'love'
as if it were
still far away.

'Not much to live
for'
I say,

put down
your heavy burden
and rest
from the hard,
everyday labour
of not hurting,
or not feeling,
or hearing,
or saying or seeing.

Stop keeping
the tears at bay,
I say,

give it all up,
just come home.

One Day

One day I will
say
the gift I once had
has been taken.

The place I have
made for myself
belongs to another,

and the words
I have sung
are being sung
by the ones
I would want.

Then I will be ready
for that voice
and the still silence
in which it arrives.

And if my faith is good
then we'll meet again
on the road
and we'll be thirsty
and stop

and laugh
and drink
together again

from the deep well
of things as they are.

ONE DAY *'One day' was written many years ago, and over those years, I have always been pleasantly surprised, both by its simplicity and the way it continues to represent the simplest possible gift at the heart of any legacy I might leave, most especially the line - 'And the words I have sung are being sung by the ones I would want.' In laying out the book, the poem kept calling to me to be included amongst all the new work; so as not to be disobliging, I have heeded the call.*

Auguries

They have happened all your life,
the bird tapping at the dawn window
with that message from your mother,
telling you through a half sleep,
you were living in a strange
new parallel, both on your own,
and accompanied now, along ways
you could only begin to imagine.

They have happened by night
with or without your seeing or knowing,
all the stars turning above you round
the fixed true north where you slept,
and you at the center of every turning,
dying through all the layers of your dreaming,
to find yourself, each morning, through
all the creative undoing and drama,
nested at the heart of the pattern.

They have happened in every
first glimpse through a light-filled
afternoon window, needing only
the briefest look into the heavens,
grey or blue, to see clouds spilling
across an open sky, all come to find you,
all wanting to make themselves familiar
and understood, the race of constellating
shapes, clouds or passing crowds of faces

now beckoning, now warning you off,
now inviting you in again.

The intuition that every outer pattern,
dark or light can find its center in some
inner incomprehensible origin of being,
and the sense, living in this
meeting between inner and outer
of somehow always being implicated,
always being seen, always being invited,
and always in the end becoming in yourself
an omen and a sign and a revelation,
your own eyes lifted to the stars
following an invisible road and the merest
glimpse of your silhouette outlined
against the evening sky, perhaps
even now, beneath every confusion,
a beckoning life that others could follow.

AUGURIES *A word I have always loved since I first stumbled across it at twelve years old; meaning 'the interpretation of omens or signs', a word that lives in parallel to another favorite of mine: 'auspices' meaning the 'interpretations made from the flight of birds'. The way we are always, no matter our outer professions of logical thought, looking for intimate indications, for annunciations or for clues as to where we should go or how we should be. The sense, unearthed in this poem that in the end we too become augeries and auspices for others, and beneath even that, an understanding of the depth of that responsibility.*

STILL POSSIBLE

Still Possible

It is still possible to be kind to yourself,
to drop constraints and fall often
to your knees, it's not too late now, to bow
to what beckons, the world still swimming
around you as you kneel transfigured
by what sweeps on, it's still possible
to leave every fearful former self
in the wake of newly-heard words
issuing from an astonished mouth.

It's still possible to feel your body
as fully here and fully you, but not
quite your own, to find you can live
both entirely as yourself and in
the lovely anonymous multitude
of elements around you, that you
have always been a brother and sister
to the clouds beyond the window;
or have lived your secret, unspoken
marriage with the pale blue sky
for more years than you could ever
remember; and that you have always
been proud to be, through all
your difficulties, a loyal companion
and friend to the foaming tide,
coming and going, appearing
and disappearing with you,
and for you, day after day
on the ceaseless shore.

It's still possible amongst all the never-ending
movement to hold the necessary anchorage,
while having a mind for the long migration,
to be ready to up and go and then surprisingly,
be gone.

It's not too late to imagine that the days
to come are the lost children you are still
to bring to birth and bring to maturity,
and that you are ready once more to be
selfless on their behalf, setting them to rights
when they fall, listening when they lose
faith, being that mother or father,
who through all their difficulties,
gives the gift of constant witness.

It's still possible to intuit a magnificent,
individual arrival, that brings you still
closer to the accompanying faraway crowd;
to live bravely and always, as someone said,
to the point of tears, to realize that you
have always had your life shattered
and your heart broken and your faith
tested by loving too much and too often
and that all along, it was never too much
and never too often, and that you were
never, ever, fully broken.

No, it's still possible to feel that spring
is in the air, to intuit these days
as pilgrim days: that these are mornings
for setting out and setting off,
early hours when new stories
have already begun, mornings
to understand that you are now living
fully in some secret parallel
where you can just as well
go anywhere by going nowhere,
when you can stay at home
and find in any given hour or day,
in the quiet kitchen, the just culmination
of a practiced sincerity, when you can learn
the daily minutiae of giving up
and giving in; the beautiful but necessary
fasting into submission, of resting
through not doing, or not eating
or not hating, or not taking, or not
judging too quickly, of learning how easily
you can free yourself and how easily you can
forget who needed to be impressed
and who needed to be punished,
and most of all, recounting who you
needed to forgive so bravely, for hurting
you so deeply: yes, to practice every day,
the difficult art of being proudly abstemious
but disarmingly generous; of learning
to entertain the unsettling truth;

that from the very beginning, through all
your difficulties, you have been learning
to pass on every single thing you ever earned
and every single thing you never fully
deserved, back to those who have
never found it in their power to receive.

Yes, it's still possible not to hold so tightly
to what you think is true, to bend your head
and assume humility beneath the eaves
of a still spreading sky, to feel in the rain
upon your upturned face, how you have
always been friends with the distant
horizon, no matter how far and how
faint its call.

Yes, it's still possible to be a soul
on its way to a beautiful, beckoning
and bountiful somewhere,
looking for the gift you will bring back
to the time of your birth, so that
you can start living again, from the very
first moment you came into this life,
but this time with the cleaner, earned
simplicity of knowing what it has taken
you so long to learn: to ask for forgiveness
by being forgiveness: to live more
generously, by greeting yourself
more generously, and then to dance

more bravely, to speak more suddenly,
and with a free heart, to undo as you go
all you do wrong, and to right the wronged
and unsettle the self-righteous, sharing
the secret to happiness with everyone.

Yes, oh yes, it's still possible to taste
the natural God-given sweetness
in every cloud in the sky, in every little
you eat; in every breath that you take,
in every hand that you touch, in every day
that you wake, in every tear that you shed,
in every voice still waiting to call you,
in every once solid, immoveable door,
now calling you through; and in every
single blessed moment turning to the next.

It's still possible to fully understand
you have always been the place
where the miracle has happened:
that you have been since your birth
the bread given and the wine lifted,
the change witnessed and the change itself,
that you have been all along,
a goodness that can continue
to be a goodness to itself.

It's still possible in the end
to realize why you are here
and why you have endured,
and why you might have suffered
so much, so that in the end,
you could witness love, miraculously
arriving from nowhere, crossing
bravely as it does, out of darkness,
from that great and spacious stillness
inside you, to the simple,
light-filled life of being said.

STILL POSSIBLE *Something of a narrative epic that, even as I wrote it, seemed to contain its own unstoppable inner momentum; an inner wave form that I rode morning after early morning, while outwardly immobile at my study desk. It was written in the depths of the pandemic, when the sense of being psychologically confined seemed to lead naturally to an exploration of energies and elements in the human heart and mind that feel no sense of imprisonment at all. Its writing also coincided with a sense of an ending and a new beginning in my own life, the last stage of any epoch in human maturation almost always felt as a breaking through and a breaking out, a tidal flood of pent up creative powers, a flood of generosity. 'As someone once said' is the French philosopher Camus, who asked us 'to live to the point of tears'. Yes, yes, yes: still necessary and Still Possible.*

NARRATIVES

Glanquin
(For Patrick and Cheryl)

The best days at Glanquin might be the ones
where nothing really happens untoward,
then swiftly does, a day when the rain beats
just a little against the window, then suddenly
clears in the sunlight, the double rainbow
over Mullach Mór unseen outside while the tea
is handed, the bright rays only flooding the table
for a moment, then swept away with breakfast.

The best days always have a sense of settling in,
while alert to an imminent call, to putting down
the mug and setting out. A phone rings; and
a horse to be seen by the vet 'but later
in the week' says a shouted conversation
at cross-purposes with the affectionate
and puzzled mumble of someone
reading Heaney from a corner chair.

But no need to move yet, the pleasant fire
and the fug of the kitchen has us
for another hour, a child walks in,
her face shining with returned rain,
and 'tis lashing' says some unrecognized
voice from the hallway, while someone
in the kitchen says provocatively,
to move our blather deeper,
'I never did like Heaney.'

Before Heaney can be saved, thank God
the dog steals a scone from the table
and is let out the door, tail dragging
guiltily through the wet grass, where
the sky has cleared once more and
the day has mended but where
it is also clear, the sheep have tumbled
down a limestone wall and come straight
back down the mountain,
flooding the field with complacent,
white, arriving backs. But there's
no trouble, just the need to walk them
back up the mountain, back up
to that waiting horizon that has been
calling quietly all along, the dog's
forgetful tail lifted again
and the tongue lolling in anticipation.

We walk out the door in boots and jackets,
faces lifted to catch the light, and hear
the faint voice of a woman behind us,
'May God be good to us again
with a day like this, and all of us safe.'

An old blessing for our skeptical days,
but in it, the newly blossoming sense
of a proper cure: of hearing
just at the moment of setting off,
the right word at the right time,

after a long hard winter, even if
only half-heard and even if it
said and meant for someone else,
and then, in the bracing air
our mutual acknowledgment and wry
smiles outside the door, the two of us
having heard it together, while haloed
above us the gift of the mountain
captivating and beckoning, at one
and the same time, framing the miracle
everyday sight of a dog standing,
outlined by spring light, leaning intently
beneath the hills, eyes a-set,
all a-glimmer for the flock.

Skellig Michael

You wouldn't want to arrive at Skellig Micheal
too early in your life, crossing those waters
where the monks spread their nets, casting
for the shoaling essence of their own souls,
and not have a clue as to what you were seeing,
you wouldn't want to arrive there, barely out
of your twenties under the youthful impression
you had made the same commitment.

No, tiptoe quietly back across all the years,
into your young breathing body and thinking
of the island, tell yourself now,
what you could not tell yourself then,

and admit you wouldn't want to navigate
that short slate-green stretch of water
thinking you'd gone the extra spiritual mile,
you wouldn't want to think you had
actually left the too solid foothold
of your just emerging life, and looking back
after all these years you wouldn't want
that younger self to think they had understood
the island, as you understand it now
and as the monks had understood it,
the hum in every beehive home
still resonant with silent prayer,
the island beneath them sailing
to heaven through the storm wrack
of a winter's night, and the chant below

the chapel ceiling holding every
windswept star in place, you wouldn't want
to look back on your younger self
that particular winter's morning,
approaching the island alone,
a gleaming mirage of raw light
above the sea smoke, and tell him,
he was in no way able for the revelation.

You might be happy after all that your
younger self made excuses, looking out
on the glass-like February sea, that even
though the day was perfect for the crossing;
and perfect for that heart leap
from the boat to the first stone step
of the upward staircase spiraling into cloud,
that it was far too cold, and far too expensive,
that after all you couldn't afford
the hundred quid, and that you couldn't
be the only person on the boat,
and you didn't deserve the island to yourself,
and more seriously, and deep down under
the disturbed, ocean currents of thought,
that you didn't know what part
of your frightening mind you might
encounter in that aloneness,
that you were afraid in that mist,
of meeting your unrequited-self full-on,
and would wither in the face of it,

as if questioned by a powerful stranger,
one too overwhelming
and too full of knowledge, to go away.

You might be glad now, to see that young man
turn away, and get himself a coffee,
and pretend to think about it, then not return
to that strangely happy, Kerry boatsman,
laughing in the winter light, your possible
Charon, ferrying you to disappearance,
you might want to leave him standing there
in his blue overalls, as you did, empty-handed.

You might be relieved that you hitchhiked
away, trying not to look back, your young
thumb taking you quickly back to Dublin
and the waiting ferry, and then, remembering
the receding outline of the Wicklow Hills
you even so, might feel again, one of
the deepest regrets you have ever experienced
in your short life, and find yourself
carrying that ache and that loss,
the rest of your days.

But then again, looking back like this
it might lead you to realize, that all along,
and all these years you have been
remembering and holding and nursing,
and growing with the mercy of, 'not going'

to Skellig Michael, as an infinite unremitting
invitation that never went away, and never
will go away, an island shimmering
in the blue mist of your own growing body
and that you have carried through every year
that beautifully wrapped and gifted regret
given to you so physically by yours fears,
like a lodestone, leading you on, almost
whispering every time you hesitated at
any last mile, that this is where the harvest
lies, that you have spent so much
and endured at times with so little
so that you could learn to arrive anywhere,
that had seemed until then, just out of reach,
just a stone's throw away, and that each time,
in your subsequent life, at any possible
crossing, remembering Skellig Michael,
it became impossible to turn away again,
not from the island, nor from accepting
whatever help you might need in whatever
implausible disguise it might take,
and that the old mythic journey
of the ancients always ended with
this one tiny step, just the radical act
of learning to let yourself alone,
right to the end, just allowing yourself
to deserve what you have worked
so hard to achieve.

The ability to find ourselves, in our minds,
whether we actually go to the island
again or not, suddenly at our ease now,
at the top of the stairs, above the mist,
not afraid of being alone with the sea
nor the sandstone, nor the island glinting
in the winter light, while the ocean horizon
stretches on, to nothing, every memory
and every single facet of our present lives
fused as one, happy to be on our own,
not as endurance or penance but as a just
and well-earned reward, someone conversing
in parallel with the wheeling bird cries
above the cliffs, and the crowd of angel hosts
breathing together from the Atlantic air,
our oneness and our togetherness, together
as one, prayer made prayerful in every new
request, just like the salt wind come
from the west, just like its movement
seeking out stone, just like you and me,
one tiny step away from some precious
hoped for arrival, learning like the monks
in their difficult prayer, to find in humility
the mercy of a fresh understanding, to find,
even in regret, even in a miracle journey
refused, such a short way home.

SKELLIG MICHAEL   *Although I turned round from making the crossing alone to Skellig Michael all those years ago in my twenties, the island, and more importantly, my refusal to go to the island, has loomed across the broad waters of my mind ever since. It was a relief to finally name the fears that kept me from that first solitary confrontation, and even more of a mercy to understand how 'not going' to Skellig Michael has both lived in me and allowed me to complete, since then, so many difficult 'last miles' of so many, seemingly impossible journeys.*

The Pilgrim Island

Step into the boat now,
and feel the swell of water
beneath the boards.

The boatman
wants you
to join him,
and to sit
looking forward
with your
back to him,
to take both those
polished oars
in your hands
and feel the sea.

Here everything
is all movement
and a giving up
to the never-ending

rhythm of the ocean,
here the apprenticeship
is to the coming and going

of horizons
now below you
now above you
now beyond you.

The air is keen,
the green seas
immense in their arrival.

In the small
windblown boat
that seems like you,
it's understood
you might want
to be anywhere
but on the way
to where you
first thought
you wanted
to go.

Your thoughts
fretting and
fixated
over your shoulder
across the windblown
straight
to a landing
on that pilgrim island
cradled in the West.

But
the boatman
knows his art
and you can feel

the ease
with which he lifts
and falls with
the sea

the way each dip
of the oars
generates its

own circle
sent back home
through the water,

the way he makes
you familiar again
with all the rising
and the falling
you've ever done
and all of it
that's still to come,

so that when
you finally
fill your lungs
with the gifted air
and lift
the wooden oars
like grown wings

it's like settling
into a unison
with your own breath
at last

it's like coming home
to the tide flowing
in every cell
of your own hands

it's as if your arms
and shoulders
circling the oars

were the
blood-beat
of your own

movement through
the body of
a tidal world.

It took you
so many years
to credit
the miracle light,
though it always
faithfully
made its difficult way
toward you.

It took you so long
to see the way
understanding rises
from the very center
of your own body
everyday and luminous,
from arriving waves
of what only seems
like the ordinary.

But you know now
the strength
of those arms
you were given,
you know now
the immensity
of the forces
coming and going
in your own tidal heart,
the way you have always
been the current
and the great sea
moving through,
always the one
able to somehow
give and receive
always the one looking
for something
to call you on
amidst all

the difficult calls
of the living
and the dying.

That pilgrim island
in the end,
just a brief passage
away,
just the other
side of a short sentence
or a sweet
blank page,
just a dab of paint
on the waiting canvas,
waiting
for you,

sometimes
like a patient lover,
other times
like a future life
unable to be still,
stealing from its past
a brief kiss
from your
unsuspecting self.

Through it all,
the island always

floating,
like an invitational
outline in the
dazzling light,

one you
know so well now,
your pen
cradled by your hand

like the polished wood
of a banked oar,

an island, you
are glad to say,

as you sit
surrounded by light
looking out to the
west,
and setting to your
work,

you could be
out to, and
back from,
in a short day.

THE PILGRIM ISLAND *encapsulates the physical experience of journey and return that occurs in writing even a few lines of poetry. It is the artist's testimony to a certain learned skill and surety. Such surety however, never keeps us fully from the waiting perils of any sea waiting to be crossed. Like the literal handling of an Irish curragh — that the poem emulates — one false move and you might be up to your neck in rough water.*

Birdsong

Years ago on a hot day in Wales,
the local bus, wending its way through
the mountains, stopped at a lay-by
where the driver suddenly turned off
the engine, settled into his seat
and opened the creaking
concertina doors.

No one asked why he had done that,
or when we we might set off again,
as if on that ravishing spring morning
it was only right to cease everything
and listen to the blackbird, just above
the bus, calling for his mate.

It was one of those moments
everyone's conversation stops
and everything has to be said
very quietly or not at all, including
the faint yet strangely radiant voice
of a new understanding
whispering in my young heart.

I still remember the quiet bus
surrounded by mountains,
the slow tick of settling metal,
the faint rustle of quiet wind
searching through the new leaves,
and the scent of wild roses

wafting slowly through the open doors,
as if it was just this morning,
not years ago and I remember
a physical sense like the might of a tide
turning and suddenly running
in my mind, of the birdsong,
passing through each lifted gold beak,
generation after generation,
the stream of sound as much a living,
begetting creature as the bird itself,
the blackbird brought to life
each year through the turn and flow
of song as much as song
was ever brought to life by a bird.

That morning out of nowhere,
out of stopping and out of those doors
suddenly unfastened and opened
something broke out, far down,
deep in my chest, like a liquid force
erupting from beneath a wall
of rock, the spring water source
of my own flawed voice,
somehow understood to be singing
and to have always sung,
parallel to the birdsong,
bringing me into being
something like a wellspring bubbling,
and drinking from it, all at the same time.

My words and my songs
as both call and continual birthing.
Words given to me, as they were given
to those who gave them to me,
words passed down but made new,
by being carried, one life to another:
my father's grounded, arresting use
of the northern vowel, Tom Charlotte's
uncompromising dialect year after year,
a moorland breeze swept with lark song,
laughter and love, my mother's Irish,
doing for English what the English never could:
and then each and every Sunday School
morning, winter or summer, listening
with my sister, to the wild, racing freedom
of the King James Bible, untouchable
by any preaching voice; and after,
Ted Hughes, John Donne, Wordsworth,
Emily Dickinson's notes tied with ribbon,
singing secretly from behind a wall:
and then every voice from all my travels,
the muezzin's wavering call
above the Bosphorus,
floating across the ancient walls,
the breathless halt in the air
lamenting with the young girl from Donegal,
all the hidden tidal meanings flooding
my life from birth to death,
words and songs that would give birth to me

and will give birth to me as much
I will ever give birth to words,
words giving birth to life, giving birth
to song, giving birth to life.

No need then, looking back in that quiet,
to reach for a notepad or a pen,
no need to say what is already being carried
for us all, so beautifully on the breeze,
solo or chorus, it's just singing as singing
does, bequeathing its own life,
it's what we want to say,
waiting so beautifully to be said,
it's just the breath coming alive
simply by opening our mouths:
it's what the song does for you
and what the song does to you:

You with your mouth open
and about to let fly, the body flowing
with the gifted vitality of an in-breath,
what you have heard been sung every
day of your life, but has never
in your voice, been sung till now.

Just the chance, just the chance,
of making new life
of sounding a new note,
that has never, ever been carried
before, by the spring air.

BIRDSONG *I have always looked back on this 'enlight-enment experience' sitting on a stopped bus with the doors open, of a summer's day, in the mountains of Snowdonia, so many years ago, as something very difficult to explain. As my central work in life has always been to explain the unexplainable, I could never fully explain to myself why I could not explain it. After writing 'Birdsong', I understood more clearly the way songs, stories and speech, passed down through my body, from my inheritance and through my own contribution, make my identity as much as any body I might inhabit.*

Schindler's List
(For Steven)

Black and white, silvered in memory,
a match flaring in darkness, then
a background of sky above a troubled
foreground of figures and the sound
and the sight of names being tapped
black, on clean white paper.

The artist works through intriguing
symmetries and asymmetries,
light and dark, inward and outward,
memory and present experience,
for instance, recreating that
overwhelming halo of light,
that outlines every human figure,
and that every child sees,
as the outward show of
a puzzling shadowed center
we share with every single being.

For the director, directing
our eyes it's all inside
and outside, fenced off
and fenced in, open sky
and shadowed interior,
the camera moving
from side to difficult side;
from one uncomprehending
face to another.

So that to begin with, as everything
proceeds, it's black against white,
good against bad, light against dark
and we are easily beguiled
into thinking we are being shown
clearly who can love, who can't love
at all, and who, seemingly,
always loves to hate.

But the camera starts to show
what the eye cannot see, because,
the one behind the lens has made
the camera disappear.

And when the camera disappears
there is only love, spoken or unspoken,
lived or un-lived, and what has never
been lived and never been spoken
of love is the only thing we need
to make a game of killing.

And when what to begin with on a lit
abstract screen, seemed to be over there,
is now actually here:

when what seemed surely, so far away
in time, is shown to be so close;

when what we refused to see is now
all that we see, artifice becomes art,
becomes intimacy
becomes welling emotion in the dark,

becomes, beneath those hidden
and rising tears, a lit face of our own
lifted beneath that strangely familiar
heaven we call a screen,
like another well itself, in which
we can see, just for a passing moment
our true reflection.

So that when we rise from our seats
thinking we have finished watching,

we find that we have not finished
watching at all.

So that when we find ourselves
trying to walk away
from our understanding,
we see that we are still being made
to sit and understand,

how others in our lives have perished
for want of something we could
so easily have given; for want

of this inside never being allowed
to breathe on the outside,

how, in fact, we live every day
on the brink of dying by not giving.

So that in some strange and distracted way
in the city street outside the theater door,
we find that every passing face belongs
to someone waiting and wondering
as to when we will stop hesitating
and give them our hidden and puzzling gift.

We are wandering the night streets
of Manhattan like this because we
have seen what we were so sincerely
asked to see, by the one who,

like his camera, has now so humbly
disappeared, so that he can return
to the work he discovered as a child,

looking for all the fearful asymmetries,
as yet unseen, amidst all the beautiful
and beguiling balance,

looking for where we should
be truthful and where we are not,
looking to catch with his camera

what others have not seen;
the heartbreak of a secret,
and unspoken love.

A work he exercises,
and edits almost alone
through long and patient nights,

and then returns to show us again
in his shy but industrious way,

what, without his gift,
without his help
and without his eye,
we could never hope to see.

SCHINDLER'S LIST *I had never seen this unsettling masterpiece until invited by the director himself to join a twenty fifth anniversary showing to an overflow crowd in the heart of Manhattan. Then I had to confront the fact that I had never seen it because I had been most mortally afraid of seeing it, touched as I had been since childhood, by the incomprehensible cruelty of the Holocaust. Sitting beneath that silvered, black and white screen, I was not only deeply moved by the story but by the consummate artistry so evident in its making. I could sense that this artistry came through a kind of breakdown of the director's own limits, something confirmed by the stories we heard later that night in his kitchen, detailing the harrowing act of recreation it involved. This piece is a testimony to the way this director, at his very best, wields his artform, and the silent, private and nameless hours of dedication that shape the very communal and public making of what in the end, we call a film, or a movie, but that transcends in that end, and in a strangely beautiful, eternal and timeless way, any name we may ascribe it.*

The Music of the Morning Sun
(Elegy For Mícheál Ó'Súilleabháin)

You have been woken and placed
in a street walking toward the morning
sun, with both those hands lifted, hearing
the music everywhere, you are walking
toward the sea, though you do not know
exactly where you are, though you do not
know what an extraordinary city this might
be, but you can see above you the ruffling
tessellation of leaves against the sky; you
can hear the birdsong and the exuberant
note of a ship's horn and that particular pale
reflection a sea can make above its calm
sunlit self, telling you it is there and also
that it is just beyond you, over the high
buildings of the waking town.

You can see and hear so clearly now,
you can see and hear music everywhere
and you understand at last how you have
always heard music everywhere, but now
you hear the essential incantatory
invitation in all things, you understand
the wordless music of all words;
and that through all the years of practice
and playing and secret praying, that
you never minded not knowing
as you played, knowing as you did
that whenever you played music
you played as a wanting-to-know

miracle amongst other miracles,
all wanting to know you,
and all wanting to hear you
and like your music, you have
achieved the unachievable, you have
become unclassifiable, un-nameable
and free; people walking toward you
see every line in your upturned face,
people walking behind you find
a happy silhouette, sometimes a man,
sometimes a young woman,
walking out on a first spring day,
someone, no matter their outward form
with a rhythm in their step,
haloed by the sun, called by every
distant strain of notes.

You are on your way somewhere,
drawn by an air you are just beginning
to sing yourself, though you do
not know fully where you are going,
though you do not know anything
anymore, though you only know
you can walk, you can talk, you can
wave a cheery hello to complete
and utter strangers, overwhelmed
as they are by your untrammeled joy,
so that you look down as if concentrating
on the inner keys of your body

in just the same way as you played
head bent as if in prayer
so as not to burden the world
with your happiness, though
you never say a word
about the source of your joy,
though you cannot say a word
on any subject at all,
though you understand only as you did
as a child, when you first sat down
before the ivory whiteness
and touched the first black keys
that you were on your way home
to the very place you find yourself now
and are just on the edge of reaching.

Walking toward the river and the sea
today, you see your hands at last
as a marvel, doing what they
have always done, you stop
in the street and open them
as silhouettes to the noonday sun,
the light coming to find you
through outstretched fingers,
and in their outline, you understand
from the very first, every last thing
they created, how they leapt like a child
from stepping stone to stepping stone
as easy and as nimble as dancers.

Your hands, outlined by the light
of music have always been beacons:
they led every building theme,
and every theme of building,
they led the sincerity of every student,
they led your own sons through
the music of the morning light,
filling the waking house
with the unanswerable, tidal run
of sky and sea and the swelling,
rising sun, and now, walking toward
this western light, this sun-lit city
by the river, you are playing
as closely and as faithfully
as you ever will to the world's
tidal reach, and as you catch
the last, faint call of the the waiting sea,
you guide the river of notes
to the last dolphin gleam
touching the sun-line of the west.

You lean forward, silhouetted
by the dying Atlantic sun,
true and faithful and outlined
as ever, in our memory,
your firm, outstretched hands
working on our behalf,
still sure of everything,
holding the chords to the last.

What I Must Tell Myself

I know this house,
and this horizon,
and this world
I have made.

I know this silence
and the particular
treasures
and terrors
of the way
I try to belong
to my work,
my loved ones
and my life.

But I cannot
know
the world
to which
I am going.

I have only
this breath
and this presence
for my wings
and they carry me
in my body
whatever I do

from one hushed
moment
to another.

I know my innocence
and against all sense,
I know something
of my unknowing,

and strangely
I know
through
all this innocence
and unknowing,
what I have
accomplished,

but for all my successes
I go through life
like a blind child
who cannot see,
arms outstretched
trying to put together
a world.

And the world
works on my behalf
catching me in its arms
when I go too far.

I don't know what
I ever could have done
to have earned such faith.

Watching the geese
go south,
I find that
even in silence
and even in stillness
and even in my home
alone
without a thought
or a movement,

I am part
of a great migration
that will take me
to another place.

And though
all the things I love
may pass away and
the great family
of things and people
I have invited
around me
will see me go,

I feel them living
in me
like a great gathering
about to go with me,
to reach
a greater home.

When one thing dies
all things
die together,
and must live again
in a different way,
when one thing
is missing
everything is missing,
and must be found
again
in a new whole,

and everything
wants to be complete,
everything wants
to go home
and the geese
traveling south
are like the shadow
of my breath
flying into the darkness

on great heart-beats,
to the unknown land
where I belong.

This morning
above the house
they have
found me again,
strangely full of faith,
like a blind child,
nestled in their feathers,
following a great coast
to the home
I cannot see.

My Courageous Life

has gone ahead
and is looking back,
calling me on.

My courageous life
has seen everything
I have been
and everything
I have not
and has
forgiven me,
day after day.

My courageous life
still wants
my company:
wants me to
understand
my life as witness
and thus
bequeath me
the way ahead.

My courageous life
has the patience
to keep teaching me,
how to invent
my own
disappearance,

and how
once gone,
to reappear again.

My courageous life
wants to stop
being ahead of me
so that it can lie
down and rest
deep inside the body
it has been
calling on.

My courageous life
wants to be
my foundation,
showing me
day after day
even against my will,

how to undo myself,
how to surpass myself,
how to laugh as I go
in the face
of danger,

how to invite
the right
kind
of perilous
love,
how to find
a way
to die
of generosity.

Photo Credits